PIANO SOLO

THE AVENGERS

MUSIC FROM THE MOTION PICTURE SO

SCORE BY ALAN SILVESTRI

Images and artwork © Disney Enterprises, Inc.

ISBN 978-1-4768-1336-3

MARVEL SUPERHEROES MUSIC

DISTRIBUTED BY

HAL•LEONARD®
CORPORATION

7777 W. BLUEMOUND RD. P.O. BOX 13819 MILWAUKEE, WI 53213

In Australia Contact:
Hal Leonard Australia Pty. Ltd.
4 Lentara Court
Cheltenham, Victoria, 3192 Australia
Email: ausadmin@halleonard.com.au

Visit Hal Leonard Online at
www.halleonard.com

STARK GOES GREEN

Composed by
ALAN SILVESTRI

Moderately

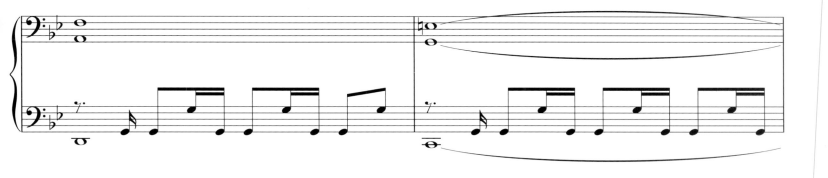

ARRIVAL

Composed by
ALAN SILVESTRI

Moderately

HELICARRIER

Composed by
ALAN SILVESTRI

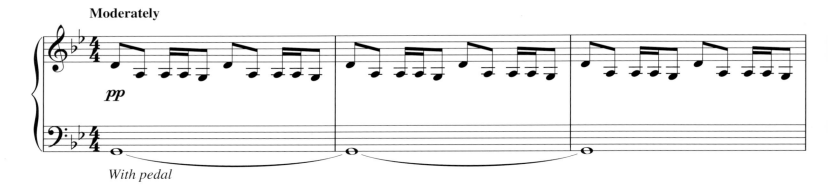

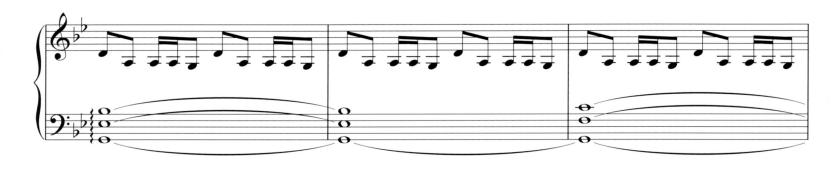

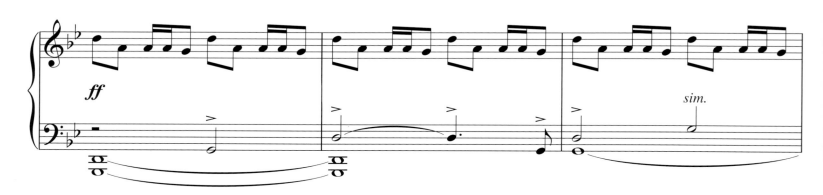

DON'T TAKE MY STUFF

Composed by
ALAN SILVESTRI

Quickly

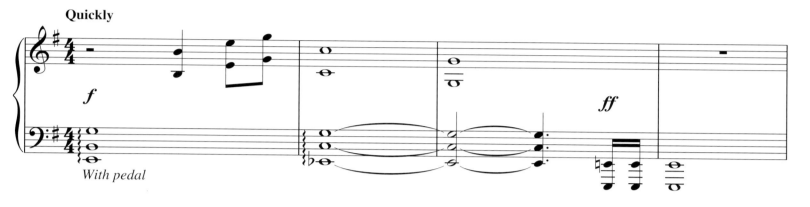

ONE WAY TRIP

Composed by
ALAN SILVESTRI

Moderately fast

mp

With pedal

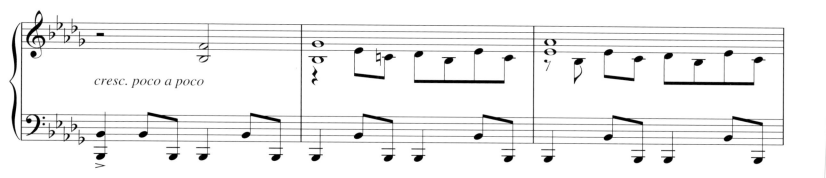

cresc. poco a poco

fp

24

THE AVENGERS

Composed by
ALAN SILVESTRI

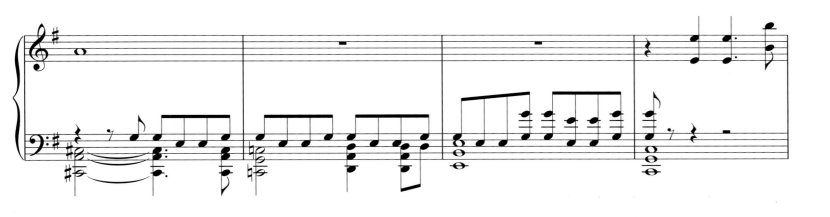

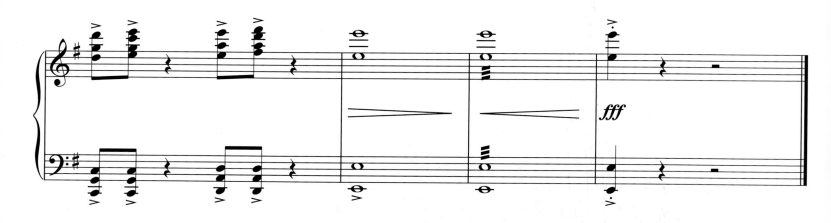